Images of
SWINDON

Evening Advertiser

Images of SWINDON

Breedon Books
Publishing Company
Derby

First published in Great Britain by
The Breedon Books Publishing Company Limited
44 Friar Gate, Derby, DE1 1DA
1994

ISBN 1 873626 94 0

Printed and bound by Hillman Printers, Frome, Somerset
Covers printed by BDC Printing Services Limited of Derby

Contents

Foreword

IF EVERY picture tells a story, this pictorial record of Swindon will conjure up a host of special memories.

The *Evening Advertiser* is proud to be associated with *Images of Swindon*, and we hope that you will enjoy the memories rekindled as you turn the pages.

Pictures are an important part of our lives, capturing those special moments. Many of the photographs in this book, selected from the *Evening Advertiser's* huge library, have not been published before, but we believe they deserve a public viewing.

As Swindon strives for the city status it clearly deserves, it is appropriate to remind ourselves of the events and achievements over the years that have made us proud.

We have tried to reflect Swindon in its true colours, capturing the glorious days of the railway; a town at work and play; good times and bad; celebrations and sadness.

The book is a tribute to the people of Swindon past and present, and we hope you enjoy it.

Our special thanks to researchers, Malcolm Rouse and Shirley Mathias, for bringing together such an enjoyable collection.

Geoff Teather
Editor
Evening Advertiser
September 1994

The Railway Town

Swindon Railway Station in need of smartening up.

The *Cheltenham Flier* became the world's fastest train in 1929 because of spectacular running between Swindon and Paddington.

Redundant boilers at the works, as the take-over by diesels gathered momentum.

A commemorative plaque being cast at the Railway Works foundry for the *George V* loco.

Swindon Railway Station during the town's railway heyday when thousands of men worked 'inside'.

Black thoughts. The last lunch break at the Railway Works on closure day, 1986.

Pictured from the top of Guardian House at Swindon Railway Station, the Railway Engineering Works were the town's industrial heart.

A few of the 6,000 locomotives built at the Railway Works before its closure in 1986.

Dinner hour at the Railway Works. From an early 1900s illustration.

The Cricklade Road railway bridge.

A new bridge over the up line takes shape.

In 1935 Swindon people donned period costume at a specially built 'station' to re-enact the birth of the Great
Western Railway.

The desolate interior of No.21 shop at the Railway Works, which was being taken over to make way for extensions to Swindon College.

A crane lifts *King George V's* 23-ton boiler during an overhaul in A shop in 1983.

End of the line. The 1,800ft-long Newburn carriage shed, built in 1937, stands derelict as the demolition men take over.

Women workers at the GWR laundry line waiting for a visit by King George V and Queen Mary who were touring the Railway Works.

The young Neil Kinnock takes a look at a nuclear flask carrier wagon at the Railway Works.

Main erection and machine complex at the BR works in 1977. The diesel engine test station is in the foreground.

Aerial view of Swindon's vast Railway Works.

Wheelmakers and fitters in AW shop at the Railway Works.

The *Prince of Wales*, then the oldest steam locomotive still running on British Rail track, was overhauled in 1977 at the town's British Rail Engineering Works.

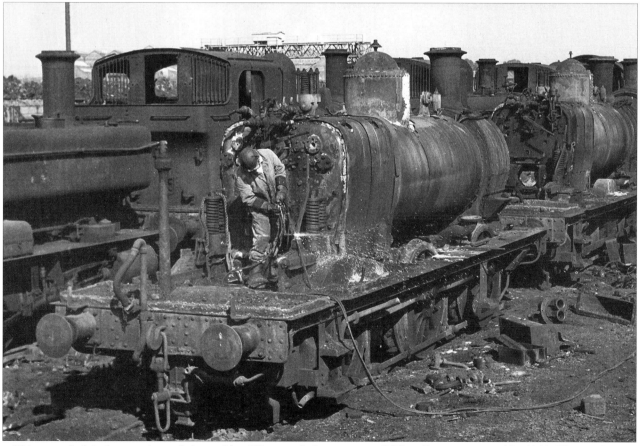

Old steam freight locomotives, their working life over, being cut up at BR's railway scrap yard in 1961. The steel was smelted down to use in building diesel engines.

A 1984 aerial shot shows the extent of the British Rail engineering complex and junction lines.

The *King George V*, two 'Warship' class diesels and a Hymek diesel hydraulic engine went on show at a Railway Works open day in 1979.

Swindon's pride. Engineers at work in the Railway Works between the two world wars.

King George V and Queen Mary tour the Railway Works.

This huge painting of a 'Kings' class loco makes a dramatic impact on the walls of buildings next to Henry Street car park.

The Railway Works' busy switchboard in the 1950s.

A familiar site in Swindon's GWR heyday. Workmen pouring out of the Railway Works at the end of their shift.

The date of this postcard is unknown, but it shows merry passengers bundling aboard a train to Rushey Platt, which is on the road to Wootton Bassett.

An aerial view of Swindon's vast Railway Works and rows of terraced houses.

A railway buff's delight.

The Great Western Railway stores department boarding charabancs for their annual outi

1909. It was an all-male event – and they were obviously expecting chilly weather.

Old Town Railway Station, which was off Newport Street.

A railway buff's delight. These four photographs depict scenes from Swindon's railway history.

Exeter Street in the Railway Village, before the Borough Council renovated the houses.

Three scenes from the Railway Works in the 1960s.

Central Swindon

A sheltered housing development now occupies the site of these Marlborough Road cottages.

Canal Walk before the Brunel shopping centre was built.

In the days of the radiogram, Garrard produced some of the world's finest record changers. This was the company's Newcastle Street main factory in its heyday.

The stables behind the Goddard Arms were once an important facility for guests.

Old Town traffic moved at a gentler pace in the old days.

The dining room at the Goddard's, formerly the Goddard Arms Hotel.

The old fireplace and table in the Goddard Arms smoking room.

A former Methodist Church Sunday School building in Regent Street became the town's Arts Centre and Junior Library. It closed in 1956.

In 1913 Cromwell Street was a busy shopping thoroughfare.

Cattle were still herded along Drove Road in 1915 when Walcot and the Park's estates were still farmland.

Drove Road used to be a rural lane through farmland.

Fleet Street and the tram centre.

A run-down view of Bridge Street, from the station end.

St Barnabas's Church in Cricklade Road has changed little since 1909 when this picture was taken.

Beattie's toy shop now stands on the site of the Commercial Hotel at the old tram centre where Bridge Street meets Faringdon Road and Fleet Street.

This former Methodist Church in Faringdon Road has lost its ivy and now houses the Railway Museum.

Regent Street, at around the time of World War One.

The Town Hall, now occupied by Thamesdown Dance Studio, used to be called the New Town Swindon Public Offices. But it is largely unaltered.

Firefighters tear blazing thatch from cottages in Newport Street.

Some of the crowds who waited for a Swindon Carnival procession to wind its way up Regent Street from the town centre.

The scene in busy Regent Street after World War Two. The Arcadia was then one of five cinemas in Swindon.

The J.Compton Sons & Webb garment factory in Station Road was an important employer of female labour. It made uniforms.

A No.5 tram proceeds up Victoria Road, headed for the Corn Exchange in High Street.

Shoppers dodging cars in Regent Street at around the time of the first Mini. The shopping centre is now pedestrianised.

Swindon's Central Mission Hall disappeared long ago to make way for town centre redevelopment.

Trade was brisk at the old Market Hall off Milton Road, demolished to make way for redevelopment.

Drove Road, when it was just a rural lane leading to Old Town.

This 1903 cartoon indicates Swindon took a dim view of the new-fangled electric light.

Swindon's old head post office on the corner opposite the Top Rank bingo club was demolished to make way for Theatre Square.

This old toll house stood in Drove Road when it was lined by trees and hedgerows instead of houses.

The GWR Park in Faringdon Road, with St Mark's Church spire in the background was a popular place for a Sunday afternoon stroll before World War One.

The Town Gardens bandstand still exists – even though bands no longer use it.

The carefully-tended flower beds at the GWR Park in Faringdon Road kept several gardeners busy.

Marlborough Road was called the Coate Road when this postcard showing the entrance to Broome Manor Lane was published. The lane now leads to a prestigious housing development.

Swindon Railway Station at around the time of World War One.

McIlroy's store before the Brunel development. Anstiss, the store on the opposite corner, was gutted by fire and later demolished.

Taking the plunge at Milton Road Baths, now Thamesdown Health Hydro.

The old Queenstown Infants' School stood on what is now Fleming Way, close to what is now a busy roundabout.

Prospect Place, long before Wiltshire Sound's studios were built.

These run-down shops stood on the corner opposite what is now the bus station in an area surrounded by office blocks.

The former National School in Newport Street eventually made way for a garage. But a commemorative stone in the wall marks the spot.

The town's main police station and the magistrates court at the top of Eastcott Hill, next to a bus garage, has now been replaced by a housing complex.

Swindon Railway Station, at around the turn of the century.

The Oxford and Swindon Co-op had a furniture shop at the top of Regent Street.

The covered Market Hall at the bottom of Commercial Road.

The Odeon Cinema, previously known as the Regent, is now the Top Rank bingo club.

This old mill at the Whale Bridge was part of Walker Jackson's premises. The picture was taken as a demolition gang was about to move in.

Sanford Street School (left) is now Sanford House, the area education office. The smaller building was College Street School.

Milton Road Baths, Turkish bath and swimming pool, now Thamesdown Health Hydro, opened in 1892 and before the time when every home had a bathroom provided countless Swindon people with their only chance of a weekly tub.

The railway bridge in Cricklade Road.

The Westcott Place junction with Park Lane is now a busy traffic intersection used by vehicles travelling to and from West Swindon.

St Mark's, the town's
Victorian railway church,
was one of Poet Laureate
Sir John Betjeman's
favourite church buildings.

The Goddard family, Old Town squires, lived in
this gracious mansion at the Lawn a century ago.
A few stones, and the remains of the adjacent
Holy Road church – which had no connection
with the present Holy Road Roman Catholic
Church in Groundwell Road – are the only
remaining clue to its site.

Shops, a pub and offices have replaced rural thatched cottages in Newport Street.

Cricklade Road looked like this in 1909.

A 1909 view of Drove Road.

The Golden Lion Bridge, over the Wilts and Berks Canal took its name from an adjacent pub where Regent Street joins Bridge Street. The lane seen to the right of it is now Canal Walk.

Terraced streets made way for tower blocks in the 1960s and 1970s as the town centre was redeveloped. The Town Hall and Central Library (left) and the building which is now Rudi's Bar are still recognisable. The white building at top right is the Police Station.

Cricklade Road bridge pictured in the 1950s.

Astill's Corner in 1903, later the site of Victoria House.

Swindon at War

Memories from 1915. The Harper family of Marlborough pose with young soldiers who were billeted in the town.

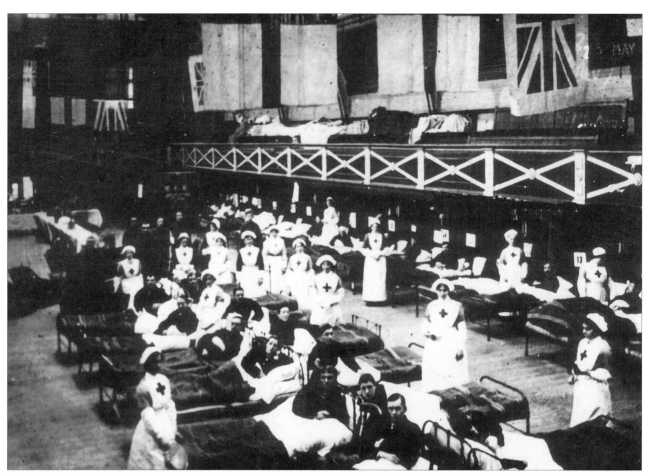

Swindon's Milton Road Baths became a temporary Red Cross hospital during World War One.

Photographed in 1936 by what is now Swindon Museum in Bath Road. The Territorial Regiment of Artillery unit,
stationed at Prospect Place Drill Hall, setting off for a weekend exercise.

Swindon didn't escape Hitler's Luftwaffe. Bombs fell in Rosebery Street early in the war as the Blitz gathered momentum.

In 1940 a German bomber scored a direct hit on terraced houses in Ipswich Street.

This Hastings aircraft crashed in a field shortly after taking off from Lyneham.

Eager men in khaki on parade for the photographer at Chippenham.

Protection unit . . .this ARP squad was pictured at the Butts in Eelyn Street, where they had their depot.

RAF crews ready for take off at Fairford. Their destination – Arnhem.

Here, and the two pictures overleaf. A lone German raider, believed to be fleeing for home, shed his load of bo

he Whitehouse Road area in 1940, and gave Swindon a taste of the air raid terror suffered by big cities.

Swindon Schooldays

This picture was taken at Rodbourne Cheney Vicarage in the 1930s and was reproduced in the *Advertiser* in 1992 as part of the Rodbourne Cheney School centenary celebrations. The vicar seated in the centre is the Revd Knapp.

Pupils of Commonweal Grammar School, pictured with teacher Miss Diffey and headmaster Dr Jones in 1933.

Swindon Schools' annual sports took place at the County Ground. These youngsters competed in 1924.

Mothers worried about danger to their children on the junction near Clarence Street School petitioned the town council for a lollipop person.

The class of 1921 at Gorse Hill Girls' School.

A class from Clarence Street School.

These lads proudly show off their new school uniforms – but which school did they go to?

Likely lads and lasses of Rodbourne Cheney School, which had been founded in 1892. The picture was taken around 1928 to 1930.

School play or tableau – or was it a pantomine? The picture was taken by commercial photographer Colville of Swindon.

Pupils as young as three were accepted at College Street infants' school in 1926 – vacancies permitting.

Innocent faces from class 2C at Gorse Hill School – pictured in about 1926.

Swindon Boys took part in the 1920-21 Schools Shield football competition.

Pupils, teachers and domestic staff of the old Moravian School at East Tytherton. Built as a church in 1792, it was later used as a boarding school for the children of Moravian missionaries, and local girls were taken as fee-paying pupils.

This May Day picture of the mixed infants' class at College Street Girls' School was taken around 1925. The children made garlands from daisies and took Union Jacks to school.

This school in Clarence Street was one of Swindon's biggest.

Pictured in 1954, a class from Swindon's Gorse Hill School.

These five sets of twins were in the same class at Ferndale Road School in 1927. They would now be in their 70s.

A class from Clarence Street Boys' School in 1921.

Class at Pinehurst in 1934-35, before they moved to the new Infants' School in 1935.

Empire Day usually meant a half day holiday for Swindon schools. This picture at Gilberts Hill Girls' School was taken in 1929.

The scene on Empire Day 1930 at Jennings Street School.

College Street School on Empire Day, 25 May 1925. The headmistress, Miss Winter, is extreme left on the second to back row.

Swindon's Shops

This well-stocked shop, owned by F.Clarke, still stands on the corner of Swindon's Lethbridge and Devizes roads. It later became Bedwin's the grocer's and until recently stocked second hand bikes.

Hope and Co's shop in Fleet Street was owned by well-known Swindon character Ray Sutton. The picture was probably taken in the late 1930s.

The whereabouts of A.J.G.King and Son's shop is unknown.

Richman's grocer's shop in Devizes Road was opened in 1914 by David Richman. He and his wife had been married for 75 years when they died aged 95 and 96 respectively. The building is now a sex shop.

This picture of Commercial Road, taken around 1964, shows one of Swindon's first Chinese restaurants.

Cars and trams used to travel up Regent Street, which was pedestrianised when the Brunel Centre was developed.

The premises of Augustus A.Hart stood on the north side of the junction of Newport Street and High Street, opposite Gilbert's. The building was later demolished to make way for Skurry's car showroom and the Co-op Superstore now stands on the site.

Brown & Plummer Ltd's bottling plant in Milton Road kept women workers busy in 1923.

The date of this picture postcard of the shopping centre is unknown. But few townspeople had telephones when it was taken. According to the caption, McIlroy's 'phone number was Swindon 21.

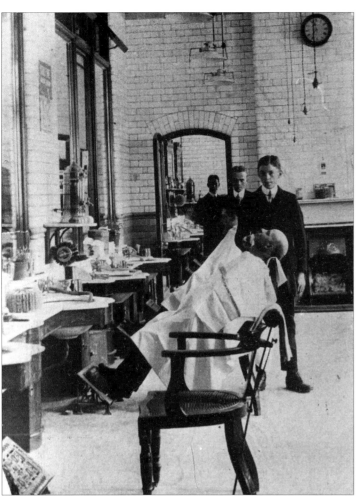

A shave and a short back and sides at the Hairdressing Rooms at what is now Thamesdown Health Hydro and used to be the Milton Road baths.

How much is that doggie in the window? Hinders pet shop at the top of Commercial Road in the 1950s.

There were bargains galore to be had at the old covered market on the corner of Market Street and Commercial Road.

A tram and some real horsepower in Regent Street.

In the mid-1960s pedestrians still had to battle with traffic for space in Bridge Street.

Havelock Street's houses were converted into shops.

The corner shop at 100 Commercial Road, photographed at the turn of the century.

The family have come out to pose for the photographer at the premises of F.Theobald, butcher and general grocer.

Some Royal Visitors

The Queen and Prince Philip paid a rare visit to the town in 1971.

Princess Anne was given an enthusiastic welcome when she visited the town centre during a 1979 Chamber of
Commerce October Shopping Spree.

Rain-sodden crowds greet the Queen and Prince Philip as they walk to Theatre Square.

A wet welcome to Swindon for the Queen and Prince Philip in 1971.

Princess Margaret came to town in 1966 to open the hospital which is named after her.

Arrive by train in time for lunch. Princess Margaret did in 1968.

Swindon People

Swindon's carnival queen in 1936 was Joyce Gooding. Gwenda Binks, on the right, one of her four attendants, became the mother of guitarist Justin (*Nights in White Satin*) Hayward.

William Maisey was a farmer
at South Marston. The picture
was taken in 1914.

Boys of 11th Swindon All Saints Scout Group, which was formed in 1929.

Working Party. Preparing the ground at the site of St Saviour's Church in 1904.

Here comes the bride, but the church on this postcard is not named.

Calne Rangers, Girl Guides and Brownies line up, badges and shoes polished, for a formal photograph.

Calne Rangers on parade.

Swindon people wait in Cromwell Street for a coal delivery to arrive during a national pit strike in 1912.

A Poole and Milsom family wedding in about 1901.

In 1924 people travelled by charabanc on days out. It is believed this picture was taken in 1924 in Earlsfield, London, and the clown was Swindon man Charles Hanson.

Little and large. The picture was taken by Fred Viner, a photographer with studios in Swindon, London and Ramsgate.

The picture shows a men only charabanc outing. But who were they, and where did they meet?

Carpenters and other workers at Ledley's in Marlborough early this century.

Prospect Silver Band posed for this group picture outside Swindon Town Hall in the 1920s.

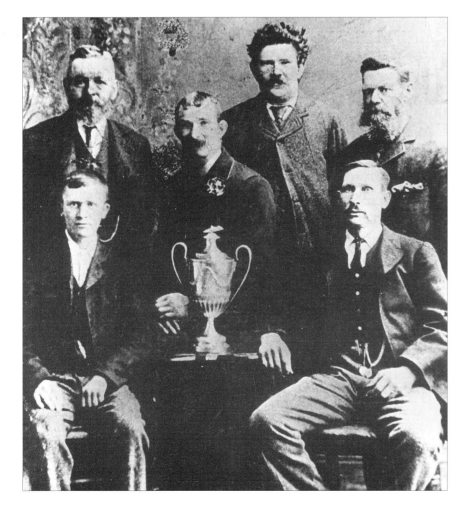

Recipients of a handsome trophy. The cup is inscribed, "To Tommie from Uncle Teddie" – but there's no indication of what it was for.

Part of the Salvation Army Band which was based at Swindon's Fleet Street Citadel. Bandmaster Matthews is seated in the centre.

This picture was taken at the corner of Morris Street and Montagu Street, Rodbourne, with St Augustine's Vicarage in the background. But there's no record of the reason for the parade.

Ceremonial opening for a new Ladies' and Gents' – but where were they and who were the men in the picture?

This formal picture of Rodbourne Cheney Club members was taken to celebrate the Coronation of King George VI and Queen Elizabeth, who is now the Queen Mother, in 1937.

The year is 1913. The fire brigade had been called to the Great Western Hotel opposite Swindon Railway Station.

The picture was taken in Swindon to mark a special occasion, but the year and what it was are not known.

Special constables during World War Two. The picture was probably taken at the old Eastcott Hill police station.

The annual "poor kiddies outing" was organised by the *Evening Advertiser*. This time it was to Weymouth.

Dressed up for a Swindon pageant in the 1920s.

North Wiltshire Boy Scouts turn out for their 1924 pageant.

In the 1930s Trevor Matthews and his band played "the latest American and Continental successes" at Milton Road Baths.

A placard saying Stratton is the only clue to the origins of these fancy dress "yokels".

The GWR Temperance Union's Swindon branch choir was popular before World War One.

In 1947 when this picture was taken, children living at Cheney Manor spent most of their summer holiday in the paddling pool at Plaum's Pits.

Child's play . . .but the identity of the children is a mystery.

Harvest thanksgiving, but at which of the Swindon area's Methodist churches? The photograph was taken between 1910 and 1920.

If this picture of Swindon Wheelers is typical, few women were serious cyclists in 1926. Only five out of 43 people in the group are female.

The Old Woman who lived in a Shoe and her children deserved to be carnival winners.

Methodists celebrate the laying of the foundation stone for Rodbourne Road Methodist Church.

Even in 1960 Swindon workers were worried about threats to their jobs. A protest march wends its way up Regent Street.

The Mechanics Institution band. The picture is believed to have been taken in about 1904.

The staff of Old Swindon and New Swindon branches of the Capital and Counties Bank Limited posed for this photograph in 1894. The boss had a special mat to rest his highly polished boots on.

Air drama. A monoplane crashed into a field near Swindon in 1913.

Pick and shovel gang – but who were they, and what were they doing?

Well-tailored and well-groomed, but there's no clue to the identity of these upright fellows.

Laying the foundations – but of what?

Mr J.C.R.Le Manais in
Boy Scout uniform. The
picture's date is not
known.

A fair was among the big
attractions for those who stayed
home during the railway factory's
Trip holiday. But so many people
left town on Trip Wednesday that
many of the shops closed.

Pity the horses. Firemen, probably from Devizes, go on parade for the photographer at around the turn of the century.

Around and About

All steamed up for the vintage car show. These veterans proudly showed off a 1901 steam Locomobile at a rally at Calne.

The car is a 1904 Renault, and the crew were clearly enjoying their 1950s day out at Faringdon.

There was plenty of interest in this 1925 Frazer-Nash sports car which was exhibited at a Lydiard Tregoze gymkhana and fête in 1967. Eight-year-old Jane Arnold-Forster was behind the wheel.

A power-packed veteran . . .but what is it? The crowd at Lydiard gymkhana and fête were clearly puzzled.

A 1911 Ellis open top tourer leads the way from Emlyn Square at the start of a vintage car rally in the 1950s.

Admiring veterans looked on as young John Cottrell tried this beauty out for size in Emlyn Square.

Dressed for the part . . .Mr S F Caudle raises his boater to a couple who admired his gleaming 1912 Buick at Wanborough Show.

A vintage line-up waiting for a Swindon carnival.

In 1970, Tom Kilminster, 20, was driving this 1937 Singer van to work every day from his home in Liddington.

The *Daily Mail* "airship" touched down in Swindon in July 1912.

Tranquil Loncot Road in Shrivenham, photographed in 1910.

Haydon Wick was still a village during the 1920s. Now these streets (*above and below*) are surrounded by a huge housing development.

A 1971 postcard view of the Uffington White Horse.

Clyffe Pypard Hill, leading from Broad Hinton to Wootton Bassett.

At home, two ladies and their maid. But there's no record of who they were or when the picture was taken.

A blaze at Garrard's Cheney Manor factory in May 1971 caused damage worth hundreds of thousands of pounds. Police said the fire – the second in a week – had been started deliberately. Fortunately all the workers escaped uninjured.

Arkells supplied the beer to this pub in Victoria Road. Greenaway and Son later had a shoe shop on the corner of Prospect Place.

St Mary's
Roman
Catholic
Church at
Cricklade.

A newly formed company of Girl Guides proudly show off their uniforms at a rally . . .

. . .while the nurses get ready for inspection.

Moredon power station, now demolished, was on the road to Purton from Akers Way.

Swindon's Art

Swindon is famous for its murals.
This one in County Road is an
impression of Arkells' Kingsdown
brewery.

Swindon Council of Social Services, later
Thamesdown Voluntary Service Council, and
its Faringdon House HQ were commemorated
by this mural in Iffley Road.

Murals artist Ken White painted this scene showing the Golden Lion Bridge. It fills the side of a house near the Whale Bridge roundabout.

Inspired by the world's top body builders, and captured in gloss paint at Swindon Gym and Fitness Centre. The picture was taken in 1986.

Breakdancers, Spiderman and the Smurfs were an important part of life in 1985, according to talented teenagers Lee Weston, John Hunt, Malcolm Poynter and Hopeton Sharp. They painted them as part of a mural which brightened up a block of concrete garages at Penhill.

The Folly, Sarah Tisdall's giant indoor mural at the Health Hydro in Swindon's Milton Road. Painted in 1989.

Famous Swindon people featured in Ken White's mural. In Prospect Place it included Isambard Kingdom Brunel; Desmond Morris and his ancestor William Morris, who founded the *Evening Advertiser*; writer Richard Jefferies and 'hammerman poet' Alfred Williams; Barry Andrews, Terry Chambers, Andy Partridge, Dave Gregory and Colin Moulding of punk rock band XTC; Justin Hayward; pop singer Gilbert O'Sullivan; Diana Dors; Rick Davies of Supertramp; footballer Don Rogers; and Councillor Alf Bown and Town Clerk David Murray-John who pioneered the town's post-war expansion programme. The mural is no longer there.

This huge paintng of a 'Kings Class' loco makes a dramatic impact on the walls of buildings next to Henry Street car-park.

Fairytale castle and enchanted forest in a mural at Westcott Place. The picture was taken in 1976.

This mural at the Link Centre, was completed by Kim Creighton and Carklle Reedy in 1990.

St George and the Dragon
fight it out at Rodbourne . .

. . .but in this mural the Dragon
seems to have escaped.

Taste of the East . . .This mural appeared
over a restaurant in Victoria Road.

This wall painting was in a house in Robisher Drive, Walcot.

Thamesdown council artists Mel Jones and Kim Creighton came up with this heavenly idea for brightening up a town centre site construction site in 1985. Offices belonging to Allied Dunbar now stand there.

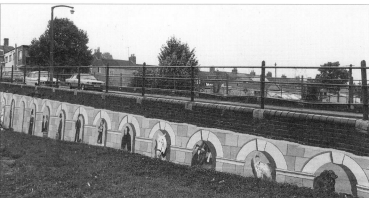

A series of murals
in Cambria Bridge
Road gave a
flavour of
Swindon's past.

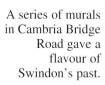

Sporting Swindon

Most of this Chiseldon pub team's footballers worked for the land-owning Calley family. The Calley mansion is now the offices of Sir William Halcrow.

This Wootton Bassett team played on a ground where a Coped Hall garage now stands.

Army footballers, their mascot – and their linesman.

This was the Christ Church football team during the 1923-24 season.

The smiling soccer players are the Clarence Street Juniors. The season was 1927-28.

Taken the year before the outbreak of World War One . . .The St Philip's Church, Stratton, Brotherhood football team.

Clarence Street School was serious about competitive sport. These were the stars of its victorious 1926-27 football team.

Sanford Street School football team of 1923-24.

Swindon Town Football Club had its headquarters at the Eagle Tavern in 1895. The picture decorated an old tobacco tin.

This was the Christ Church football team's official picture for 1912.

These likely lads played for Swindon Victoria Athletic Football Club in 1899-1900.

The Old Swindon United team which competed in the Swindon and District League in 1900-01.

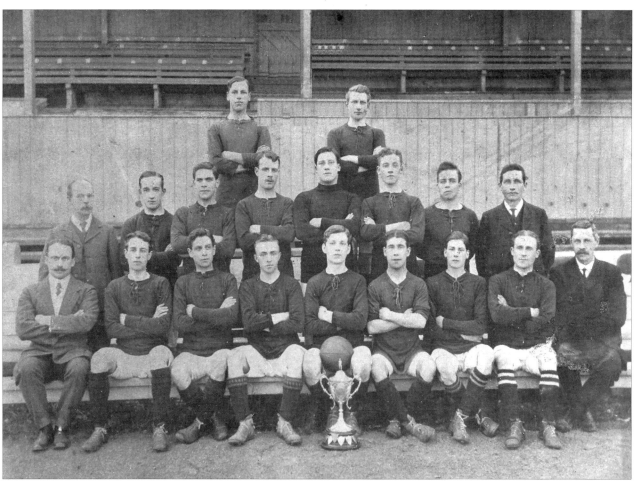

Swindon Town Juniors won the Swindon Senior Cup in the 1911-12 season.

A local Swindon school side in 1921-22 – but their names   are unknown.

Swindon Town pictured in 1911-12, around the time they were enjoying some good runs in the FA Cup. Second from the left of the front row is Swindon's famous England international forward Harold Fleming. The son of a clergyman, Fleming refused to play football on a Christmas Day or Good Friday. He later became proprietor of a football boot manufacturing company in Swindon and also played cricket for Wiltshire.

Swindon Town's finest hour came in 1969 when, as a Third Division team, they went on to collect the Football League Cup, beating the mighty Arsenal by three goals to one. Here, Roger Smart scores in the 34th minute. Don Rogers was the scorer of the other two.

More action from the League Cup Final as Swindon's Peter Noble challenges the Arsenal goalkeeper, Bob Wilson (later to become a TV sports presenter).

Swindon Town, pictured during the 1980-81 season.

The Inter-Town Team were joint holders of the Swindon Wednesday League championship in 1922-23, and champions in 1924-25 and 1925-26.

Cricketers, but who were they and when did they play?

The time was the 1920s, and the subject is probably a Swindon golf club.

Swimmers from Clarence Street School won a relay cup in 1907.

Carefully posed photograph of a couple of professional fighters. The year is unknown.

Swindon Wheelers, pictured in 1926 when cycling was in its heyday.

Winning wheelers. But there's no record of the year, or who they were.

The Euclid Street netball team in 1941.

Sit up straight, girls! The Swindon Drill Hall Gymnastic Society with their instructor.

Swindon Chamber of Commerce went to the Wye Valley for their annual outing in 1926. For 25 shillings (£1.25) they had lunch, a boat trip, tea, dinner and entertainment, and travelled home to Swindon by special express train.

Subscribers

Paul Adams
W H J Adams
Marie Affleck
Salma T Aitcheson
H Akers
Mr James Akers
Roy Allbright
Jean Allen
A G Andrews
Mr & Mrs D D Appleford
E Appleford
J K Appleford
P F Appleford
Fred J Archer
F A Badham
Ray Bailey
Trevor J Bailey
Mr J S Baker
Jeff Ball
Julie Wilshire & Steve Ball
J E Bamford
Sally Barrat
Dennis F Barrett
Mrs M A Barrie
Dave Bedford
Beechcroft Infants School
Mr K S Benn
Mr A S Bennett
Mr David Bint
Neil Bird
Peter J Blackford
Mr M C Bond
Roy Bostock
Michael Boulton
Christopher R Bowles
Kevin Bowles
I E Branscombe
Paul Brentall
William Brettell
Harry Brickell

Mr I P Bridges
Reginald Bridgman
Paul Bristow
Joy Brown
Mr Colin Buckingham
M T Burns
W T Butler
M Y Butt
Neil Butters
Robert Cameron
E C Canavan
E R M Cann
Mr C J Carpenter
Mr John Carter
Leslie Carter
Mary Case
Derick Cawte
Pat Chapman
Richard Chapman
D Charleston
Mrs B Clark
P M Clark
Davis W Clarke
Mr N C Clements
Edith & Arthur Comley
G D Compton
Angela Conway
P Cook
D G Coombs
Andrew Cox
Judith & Verbena Cox
Mrs O M Cox
Gordon & Linda Crabbe
Terry Crewe
Donald Crippen
John Crocker
Mrs D Crook
D R Crook
J K Crowe
Mr J Dashfield

Brian K Davis
D A Davis
I W Day
Susan & David Dean
Valerie Dennis
Mr M G Deverill
Mr A P Dibbens
Mrs D Dodson
Ingrid Doherty
Joyce Douglas
Mr D Drew
G Duponcheele
Stefan Dziubinski
Brian East (NZ)
P J T Eborn
Mrs Esmé Edney
L A C Edwards
Winston Elliott
Richard Elwen
The Even Swindon Working Men's
    Club & Institute
Mr D G Evans
Mr & Mrs D J Evans
Mr Peter Evans
Russ Everiss
Mr John Eyres
Robert Fair
Mr W N Ferguson
R A & J V Ferris
Robert J Fiddes
Peter Field
Ken Fisher
Martin Fisher
N E Fisher
Mrs R N Fishlock
Peter David Fogden
Leslie Gair
D F Garlick
John A Gentleman
Mrs D Gingell
Shirley Goarin
Mrs S J Goddard
K Goodings

Christopher Gough
Michael Gould
Mr G I J Grant
M E & M C Grant
Nigel Gratton
Brian Gray
Mrs O J Griffin
Mr C H Gwyther
H S Hacker
Ken Hacker
Joan Haines
Mrs P M L Hall
D R Hammond
Mr Bill Hanks
Mr Frank Hanks
Mr Brian Harry
David William Hart
T W F Hatcher
Mr K T Hatherall
Mr Glyn Haugh
Alan Hazell
G Heavens
Mrs B J Herbert
G W Herbert
Ella Higgs
Mervyn Hill
Mrs U S Hill
Antony R H Hillier
Jack Hillier
Mrs Nellie Hobbs
Reg Holloway
Derek A R Horne
Edward J Houghton
Mr R C & Mrs J D Howell
Jeanne Howland
Stephen Howse
Fred Hughes
D Hunt
J Huntley
F V Hutchings
John Hutchins
Cynthia Hyde
Graham C Iles

Mrs E Ingham
David Jefferies
Mr David Jell
Alan Jennings
Mr D R Johnson
Mr D Jones
Mr D R Joyce
Mr Kalupa
Valerie Kearby
Kelly Family
Mr Don Kenchington
Betty Kilminster
Jim Kimber
Kingsdown School
Don & Christine Kinnett
P F Kinsman
J Knox
David Kral
F R W Lambert
Alan Lambourne
Cyril Larty
Mrs M P G LaTouch
Mrs Doris Law
Mr R P F Leger
A P Lenham
L Leo
K Lester
Jane & Jack Lewis
Paul Liley
Stanley Lilley
F A Linfield
Mr E J Little
Mrs P T Little
Mr J D Loveday
Paula Milner & Ted McGill
A McGovern
Shirley McGovern
Rod Mackay
Mr R P Maisey
Roger & Rita Maisey
David Mallender
Marjorie & Vanessa
W G & J A Marsh

Mr J Martin
Mr H Marvell
Ben Matthews
Robert Matzak
Roger Maull
Frank M May
Mrs Ann Meeking
Philip Mercer
Mr & Mrs I H Miles
Keith & Mary Milner
Paul Morris JP
Mr Victor Moss
Michael Naughton BEM
Mrs P Neal
Mrs W Neal
C M Nicholls
M A & C M Nokes
R Norton
Mr G Nutt
Marjorie Obradovic
Jennifer O'Brien
David H Ockwell
Terence Odey
Mick & Gill O'Leary
Barry Oscroft
C M Packer
Janet Page
R M Page
Michael Parry
Chris Parsons
Mr & Mrs Peachey
Reg & Nancy Peacock
Gordon James Pearce
R N Pearce
Mrs Rosemary Perdue
Mr L Perfitt
Mrs R K M Perry
Richard Phillips
Norman Pickett
Trevor Pinnegar
Mr W J Pitt
Geoffrey N Pitts
Jack Plumb

Joy Pollard
Nicholas Pollard
Simon Pollard
Mr John Poole
Graham & Diana Price
G H Price
H Probets
Mr David Pyper
Ann Rainey
F G Ray
David Read
David Reed
Mr Ivor J D Reens
Ann & Brian Rees
Mrs L Rees
David Reeves
Mary Reynolds
Mr & Mrs M Reynolds
S Ribbins
Iris Richardson
M S Ringham
Mrs F I Roach
Malcolm Roberts
D J Robertson
Mrs S P Robertson
Peter G Robins
M F & D A Rogers
Stanley Roper
Rosanna
Mr E Rowland
Pete Rowland
Mr Martyn Ruddle
R J Russell
Gordon Saunders
Mrs L Sawyer
Mr & Mrs Scarr
Mary & Chris Scott
Paul Scott
Joe Selwood
Kay R Sewell
John Seymour
David Shill
David W Shore

Mrs Joan Shurmer
R Simmons
Mr V Simon
Eric Simons
Mr Colin Skingsley
Janet Smart
Mr A C J Smith
Ashley Smith
Mrs I Smith
Mrs J Smith
Mr C F & Mrs P M Smith
Jonathan Morgan Smith
M Smith
Mrs R M Smith
Ronald Lancaster Smith
Royston Spackman
David John Spalding
Sheila Sparrow
Mrs B Spooner
G F Spooner
David Starkey
Michael Starkey
Mr D Stennard
Fred Stevens
Margaret Stevenson
C Stoddard
Eric Stott
Olive Stranks
L Stratton
Margaret Sturmey
Margaret & Reg Sumbler
Roger Summerfield
David Evans Sutton
Donald Sutton
Mrs Josephine Thomas
Mr Tony Thompson
Terence Thurtell
Mrs F H Timmins
John Titcombe
Mrs Phyllis Titterton
Mr J L Toolen
Mr P D Tough
Patricia Townsend

Mrs J Troy
R A Tucker
Mr D I Tuddenham
Dr Eric V Tull
H M Turner
Anthony John Tylee
Barry Tylee
Marion & John Tylee
Mr Cyril Vowles
Sue Wagoner
E Walker
Lynn Walker
Patrick Walsh
Christine Warman
Keith Watts
Pamela Webb
Mr P F T & Mrs M J G Webb

Tim Westcott
Mrs J Wheeler
Tydvil Wheeler
Andrew Michael White
Tony & Ann White
W E White
Mr Norman Whitworth
K L Wickam
Mr W Wickenden
H R Wightman
Ken Wilmer
Alan S Wing
Stanley C Wing
Mrs D Woodward
Michael William Yeo
R Zarczynski